Write the Numbers

zero

one

two

three

four

five

Match How Many

How many are there in each set?
Draw a line from the set to the number.

0

1

2

3

4

5

How Many?

How many are there in each set?
Write the number in the box.

Write the Numbers

six  6

seven  7

eight  8

nine  9

ten  10

Match How Many

How many are there in each set?
Draw a line from the set to the number.

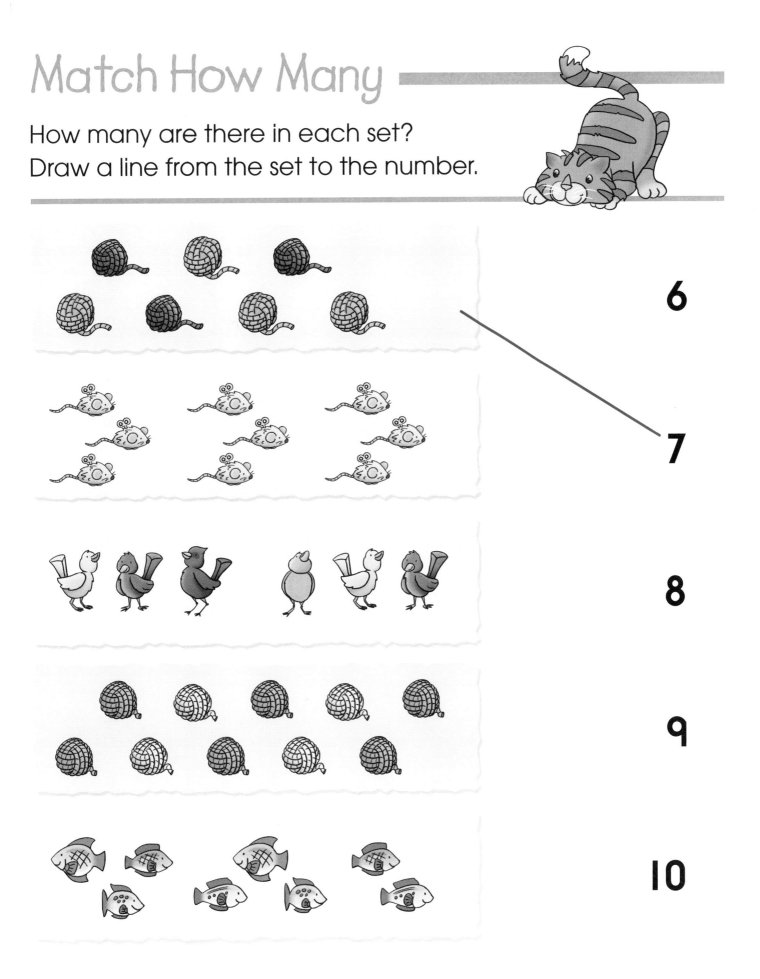

6

7

8

9

10

How Many?

How many are there in each set?
Write the number in the box.

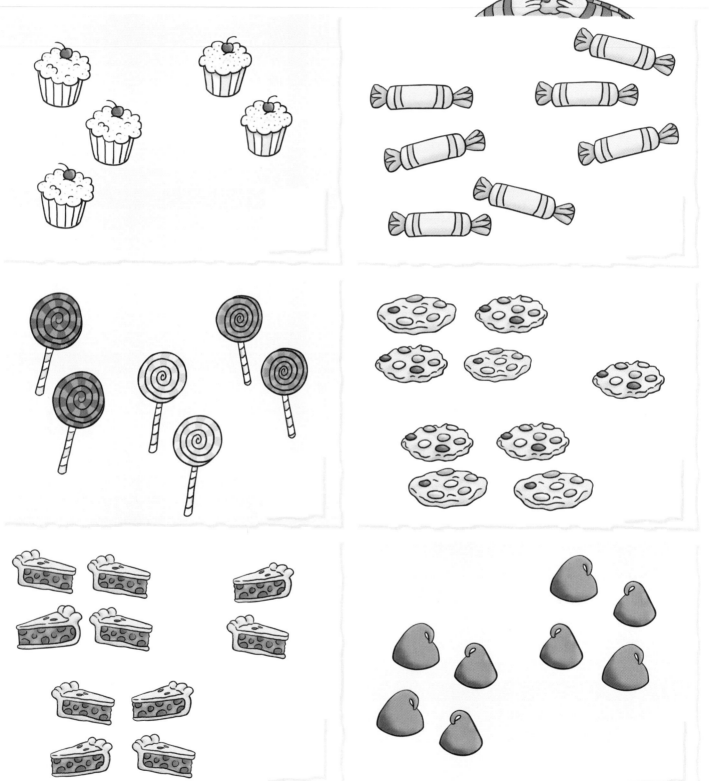

Color How Many

Read the number. Color that number of objects.

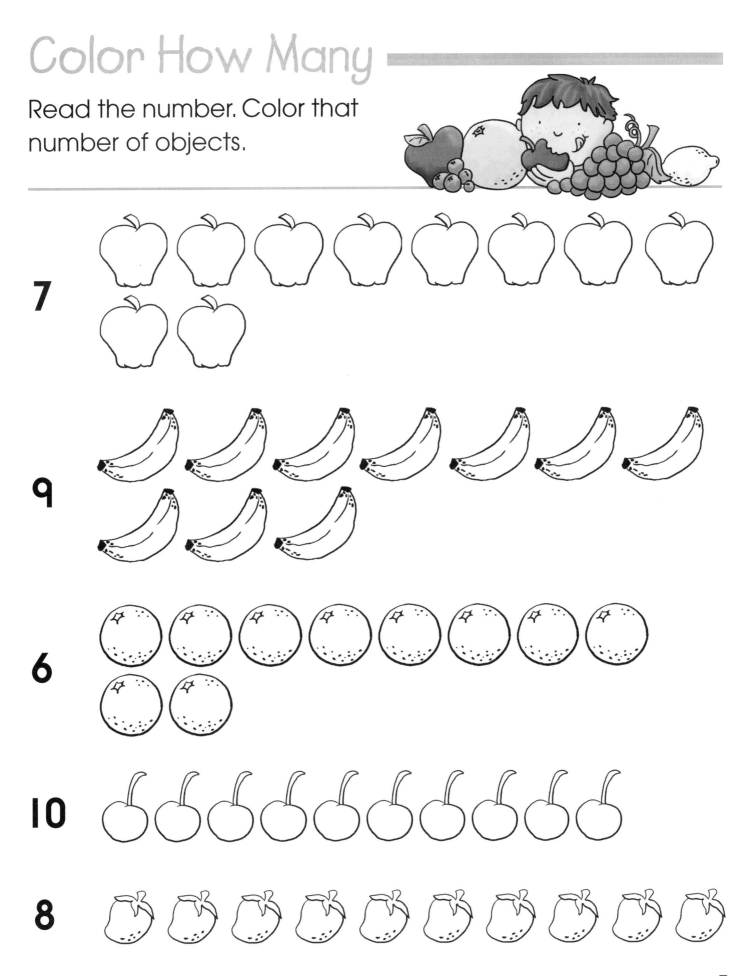

7

9

6

10

8

Find the Numbers

The numbers **0, 1, 2, 3, 4, 5, 6, 7, 8, 9,** and **10** are hidden in the picture. Find the numbers and circle them.

Count, Color, Write

Count the objects in the set.
Color the number of blocks.
Write the number.

Count **Color** **Write**

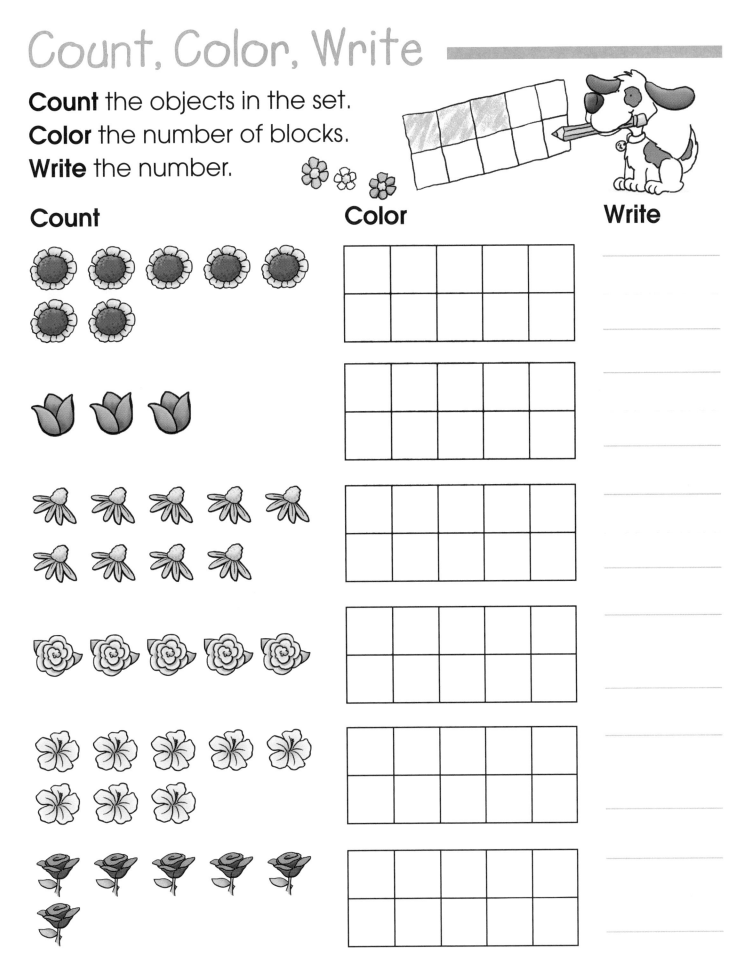

Numbers 0–10   9

Write Missing Numbers

Write the missing numbers.

0 1 2 ___ 4 5

___ 1 ___ 3 ___ 6

___ 4 ___ 6 ___ 8

4 ___ ___ 7 ___ 9

___ ___ 6 ___ ___ 10

Dot-to-Dot

Connect the dots. Begin at **0**.

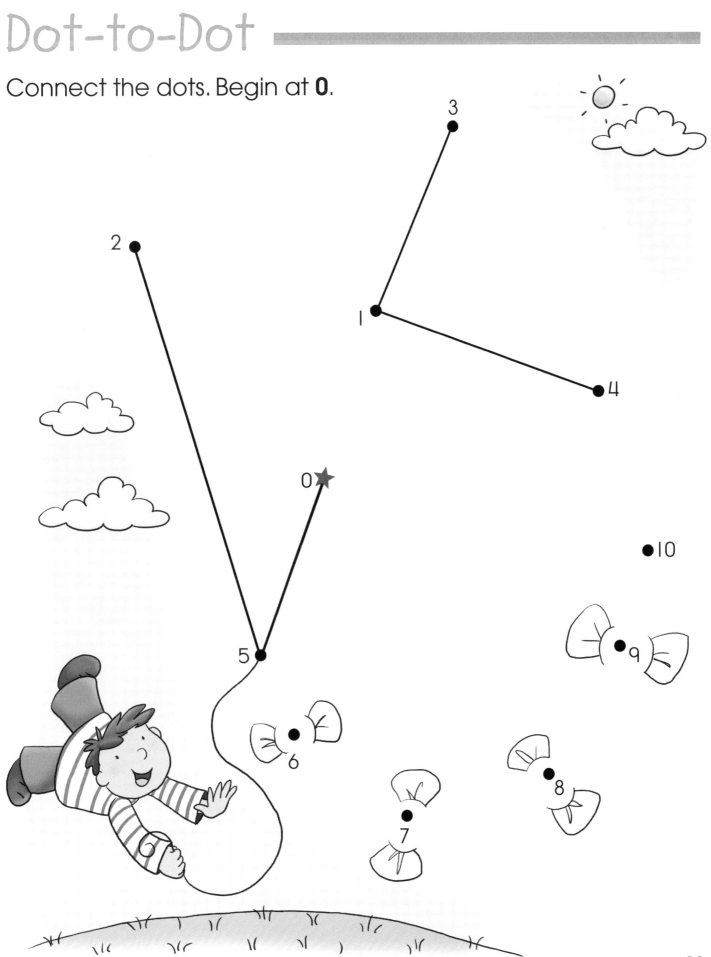

Order numbers 0–10   11

Which Number Is Greater?

Match the different objects one to one.
Which set has **more** objects?
Circle the number that is **greater**.

(3)

2

9

6

8

7

4

8

Compare numbers 0–10; concepts of *more* and *greater*

Which Set Has More?

Circle the set in each box that has the **greater** number of objects. Write the number for the set that has **more** objects.

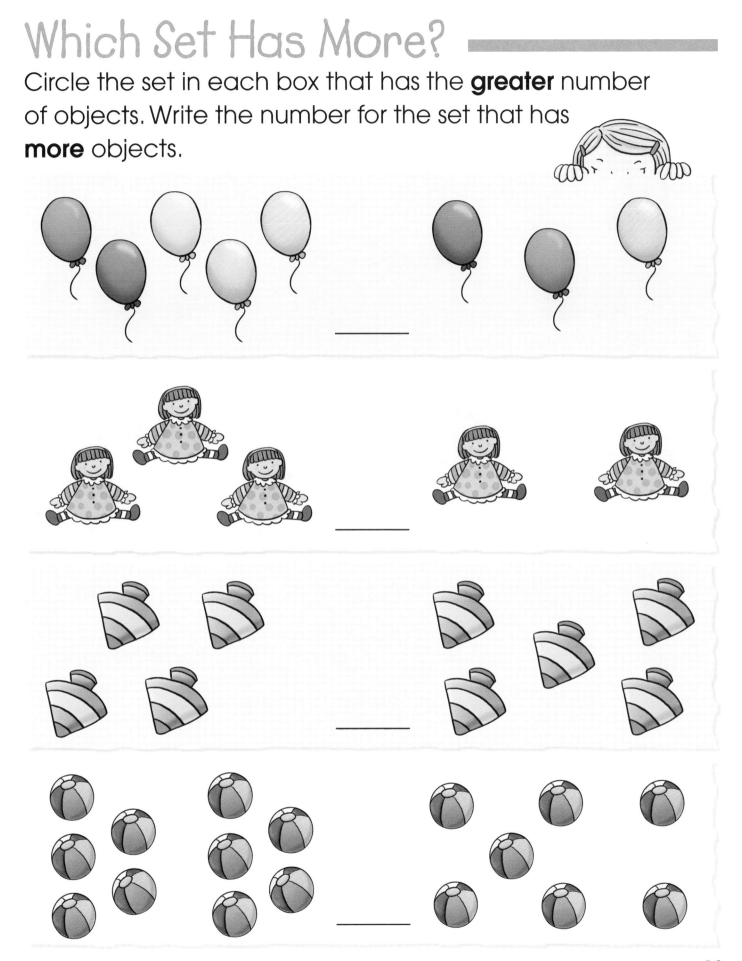

Compare numbers 0–10; concepts of *more* and *greater* 13

One More

Circle the set in the box on the right that has **1 more** object than the box on the left.

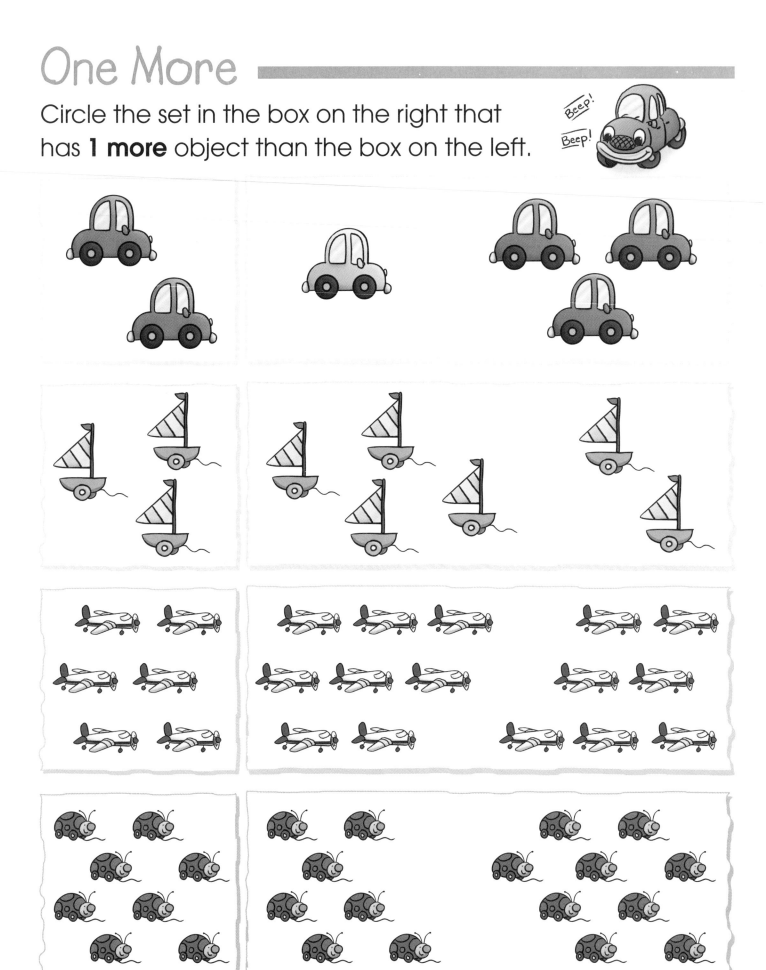

Compare numbers 0–10; concept of *one more*

Two More

Circle the set in the box on the right that has **2 more** objects than the box on the left.

Which Number Is Less?

Match the objects one to one.
Which set has **fewer** objects?
Circle the number that is **less**.

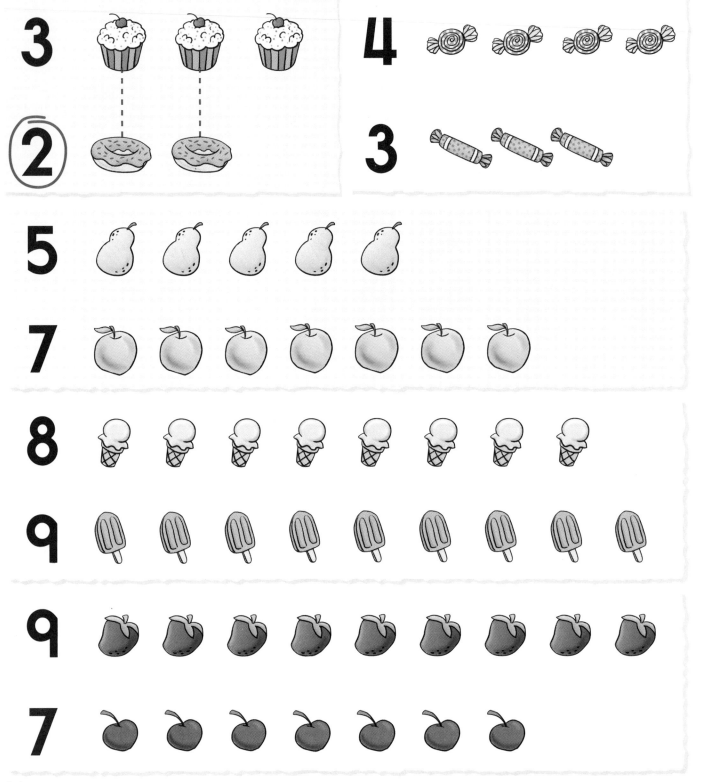

3

(2)

4

3

5

7

8

9

9

7

Compare numbers 0–10; concepts of *fewer* and *less*

Which Set Has Fewer?

Circle the set in each box that has **fewer** objects.
Write the number for the set that has **fewer** objects.

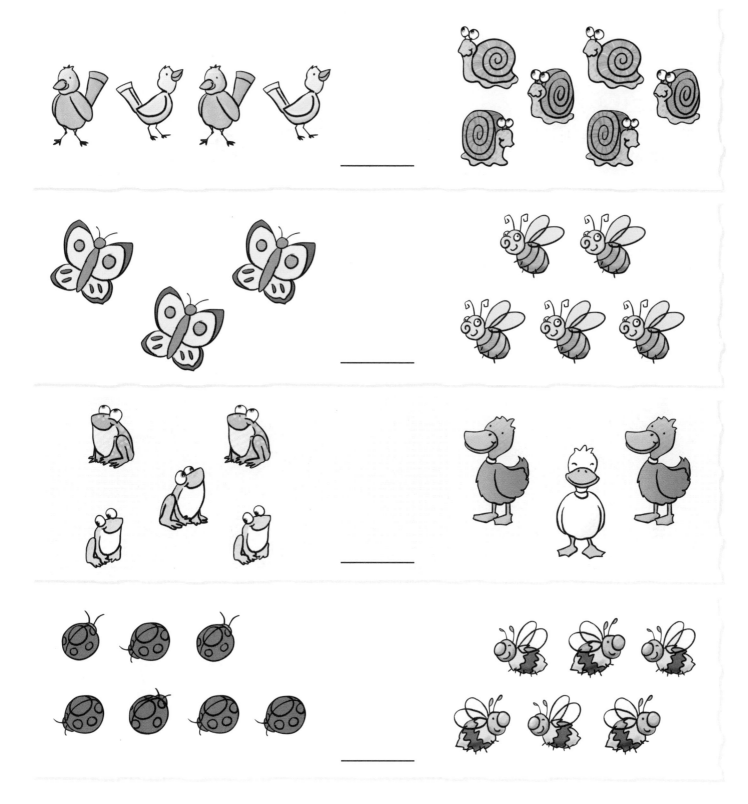

One Less

Count the number of objects in each set. Write the number.
Circle the number that is **1 less** in each box.

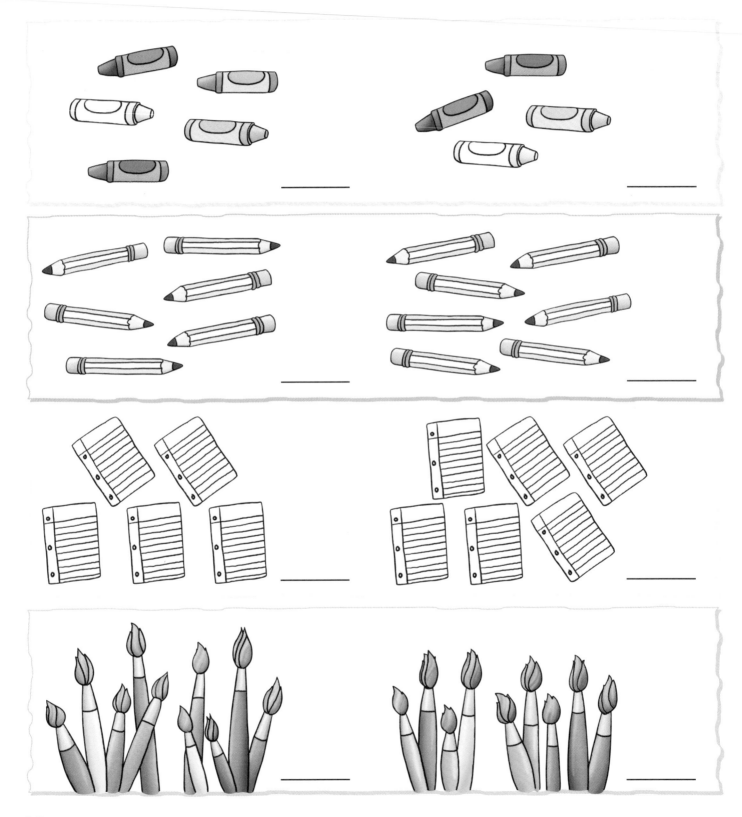

Compare numbers 0–10; concept of *one less*   © School Zone Publishing Company

Two Less

Circle the set of objects in the box on the right that has **2 less** than the box on the left.

Write the Numbers

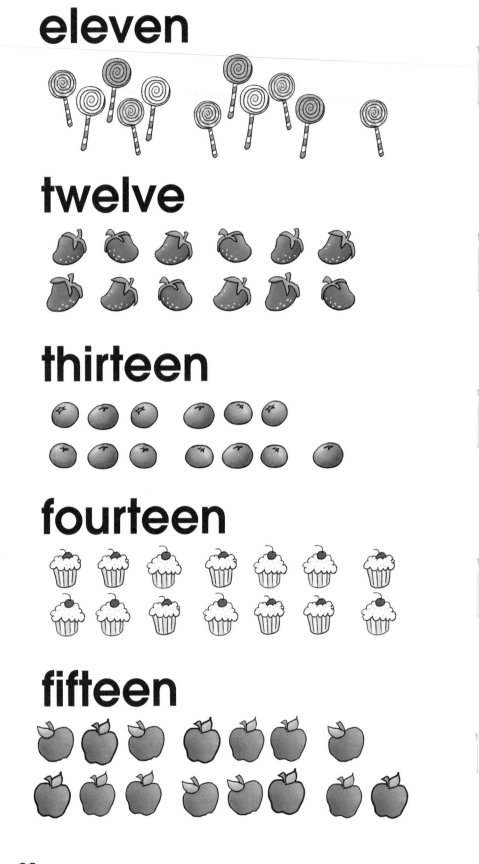

eleven

twelve

thirteen

fourteen

fifteen

How Many?

How many are there in each set?
Write the number in the box.

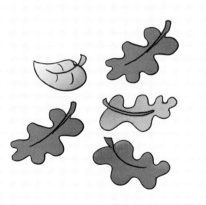

Write the Numbers

sixteen

1 6

seventeen

1 7

eighteen

1 8

nineteen

1 9

twenty

2 0

How Many?

How many are there in each set?
Write the number in the box.

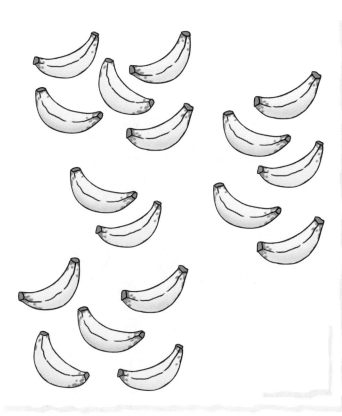

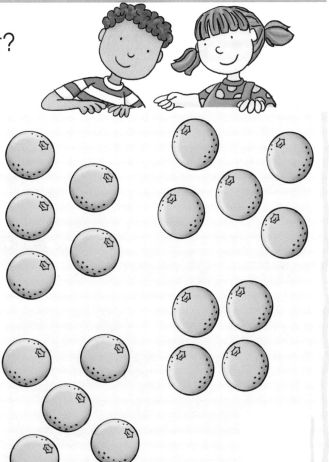

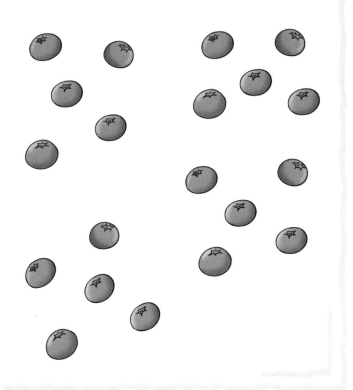

Find the Numbers

The numbers **5, 7, 8, 12, 13, 15, 16, 18,** and **20** are hidden in the picture. Find the numbers and circle them.

Count, Color, Write

Count the objects in the set.
Color the number of blocks.
Write the number.

Count	Color	Write

Draw Missing Objects

Read the number.
Draw the missing objects to make
the set of objects match the number.

12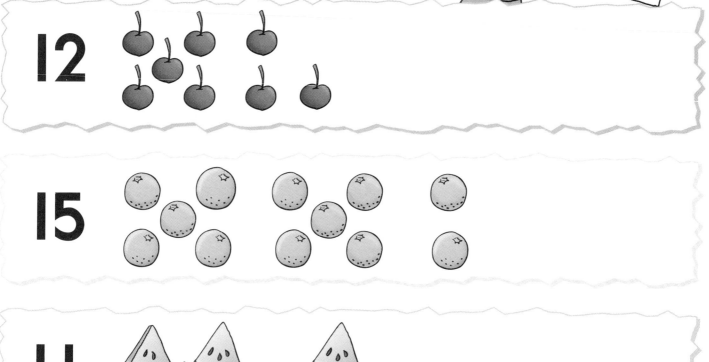

15

11

17

20

What Comes Before?

6 7 8

6 comes **before 7**.
Write each number that belongs **before**.

4 5

12 13

6 7

9 10

3 4

16 17

What Belongs Between?

4 5 6

5 belongs **between 4** and **6**.
Write each number that belongs **between**.

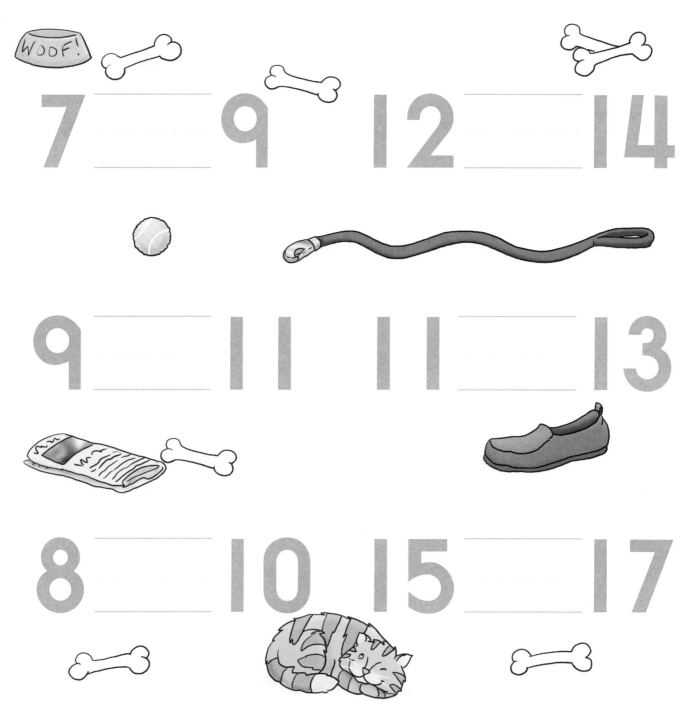

7 ___ 9   12 ___ 14

9 ___ 11   11 ___ 13

8 ___ 10   15 ___ 17

What Comes After?

5 6 7

7 comes **after 6**.
Write each number that belongs **after**.

13 14 _____

3 4 _____

17 18 _____

8 9 _____

10 11 _____

6 7 _____

Write Missing Numbers

Write the missing numbers.

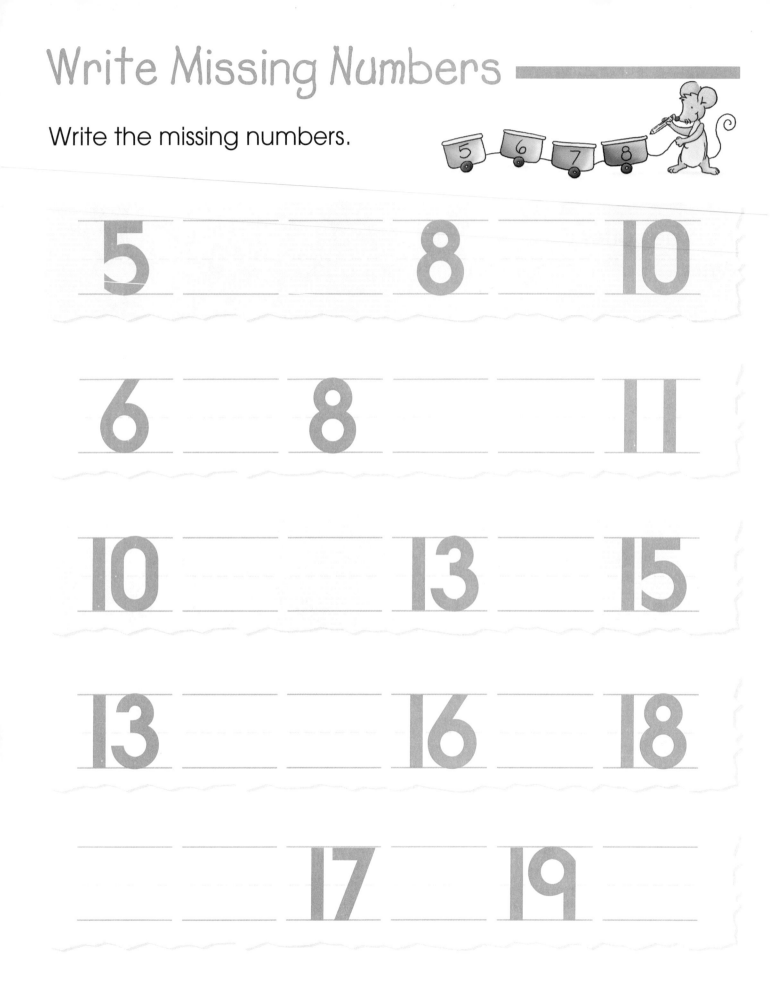

5   8   10

6   8   11

10   13   15

13   16   18

          17   19

Dot-to-Dot

Connect the dots. Begin at **1**.

Which Set Has More?

Count the number of objects in each set. Write the number.
Circle the set that has **more** objects.

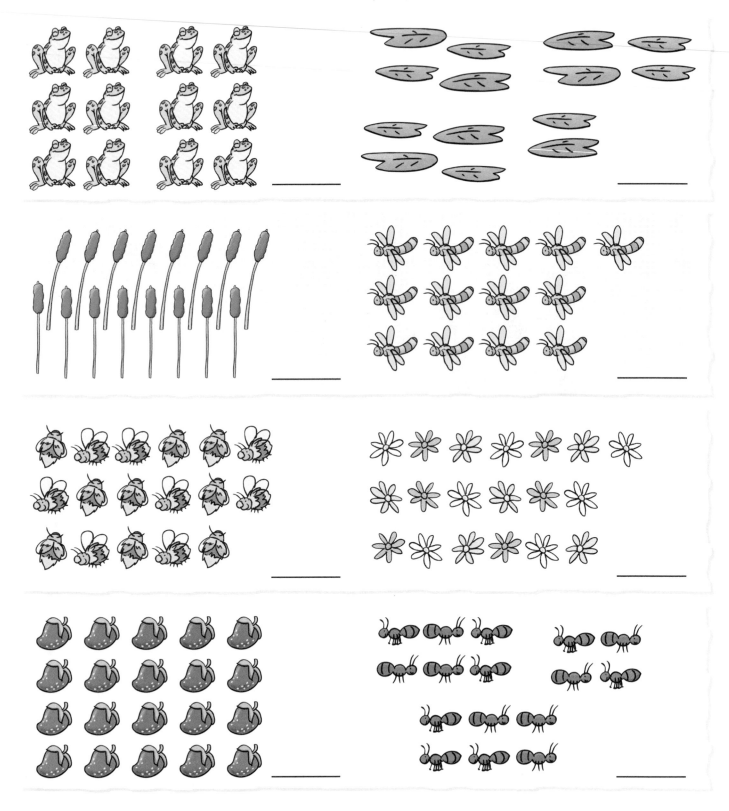

Compare numbers 11–20; concept of *more*

© School Zone Publishing Company

Which Number Is Greater?

Read the number.
Draw that many **X** s.
Circle the number that is **greater**.

13 X X X X X X X X X X
        X X X

12

7

10

15

17

9

19

Compare numbers 0–20; concept of *greater*

Which Set Has Fewer?

Count the number of objects in each set. Write the number. Circle the set that has **fewer** objects.

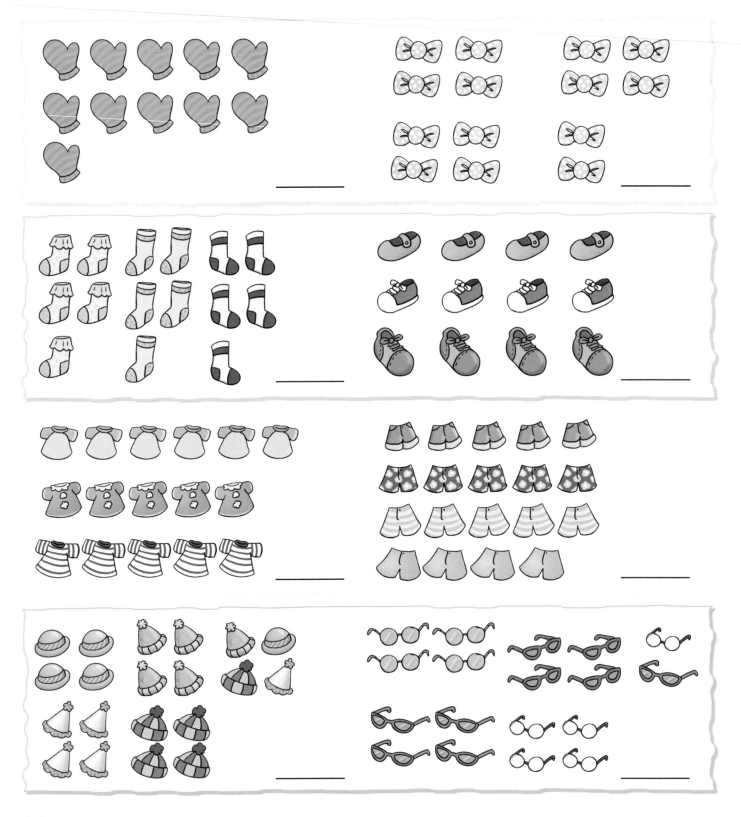

Compare numbers 11–20; concept of *fewer*

© School Zone Publishing Company

Which Number Is Less?

Read the number.
Draw that many **X** s.
Circle the number that is **less**.

9

6

13

15

7

17

19

14

Compare numbers 0–20; concept of *less*

Four Shapes

Trace each **shape**.
Find a shape in each picture that matches a shape below.
Draw a line from the picture to the shape.

square　　　**circle**　　　**triangle**　　　**rectangle**

Color Shapes

Color each ▢ 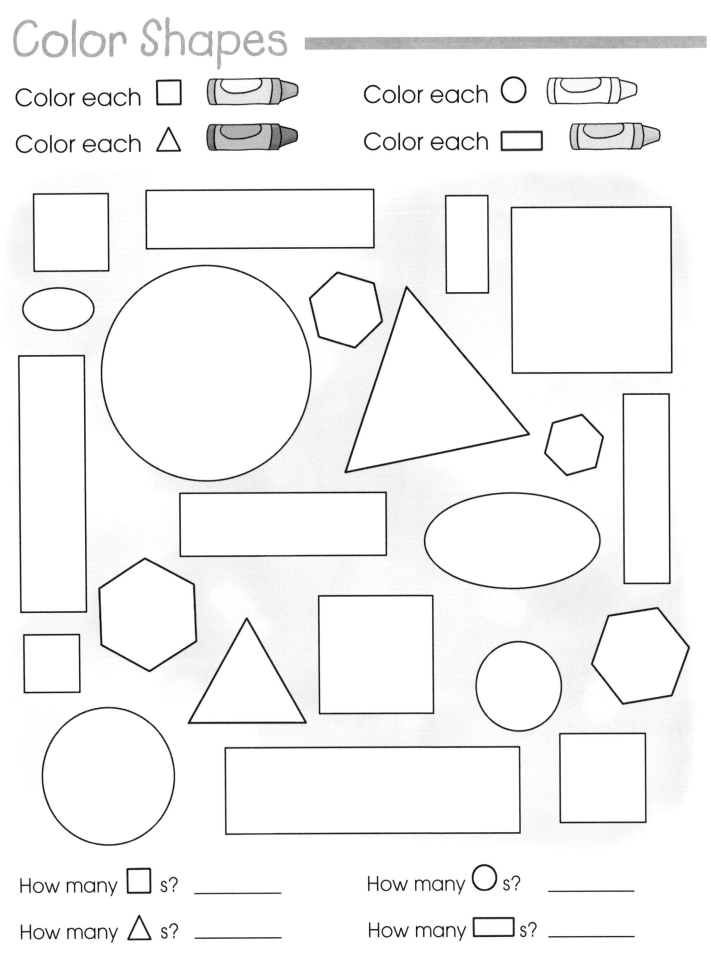 Color each ◯

Color each △ Color each ▭

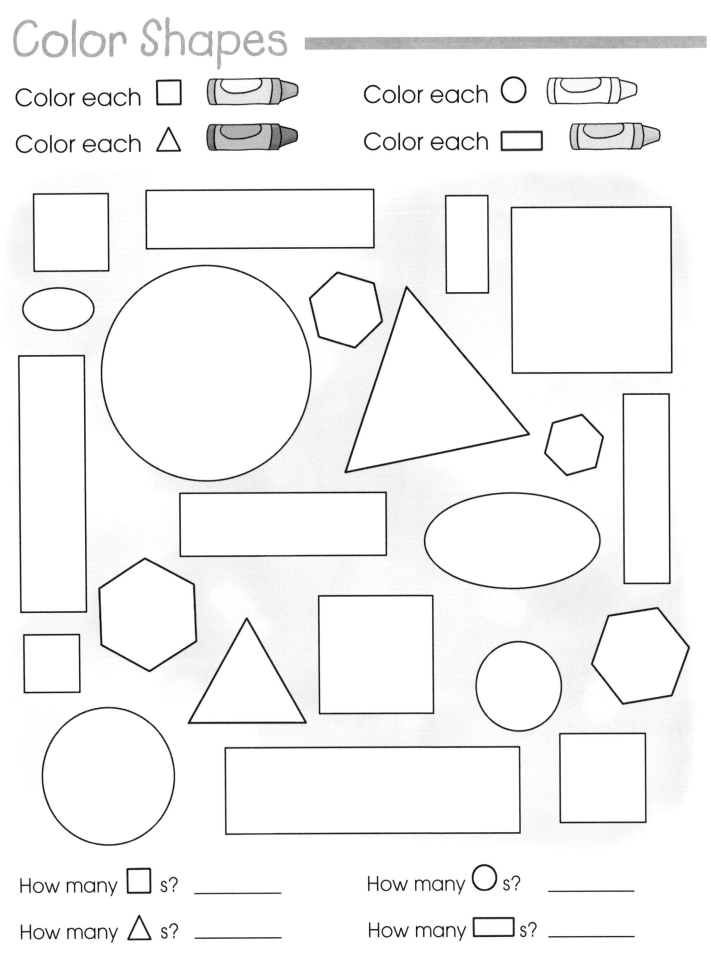

How many ▢ s? _____   How many ◯ s? _____

How many △ s? _____   How many ▭ s? _____

Geometric shapes

Draw Shapes

You can connect dots to **draw** a shape.

square   **rectangle**   **triangle**

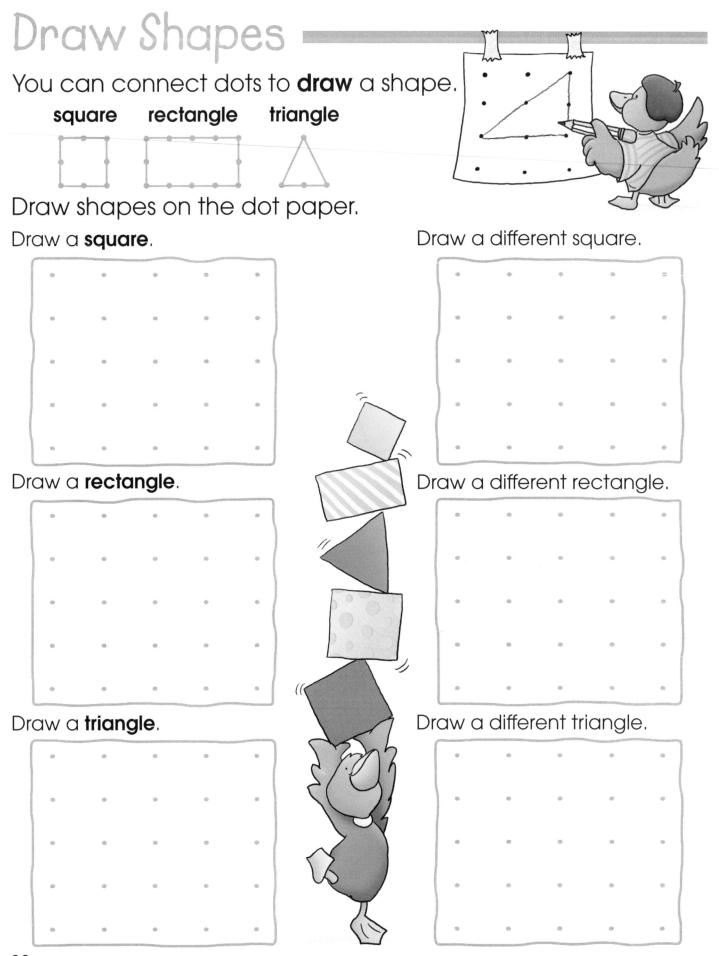

Draw shapes on the dot paper.

Draw a **square**.

Draw a different square.

Draw a **rectangle**.

Draw a different rectangle.

Draw a **triangle**.

Draw a different triangle.

Find Shapes

Write **c** on each ◯ . How many ◯ s? _____
Write **t** on each △ . How many △ s? _____
Write **s** on each ▢ . How many ▢ s? _____

Identify and count geometric shapes

What Comes Next?

Draw the shape that comes **next**.

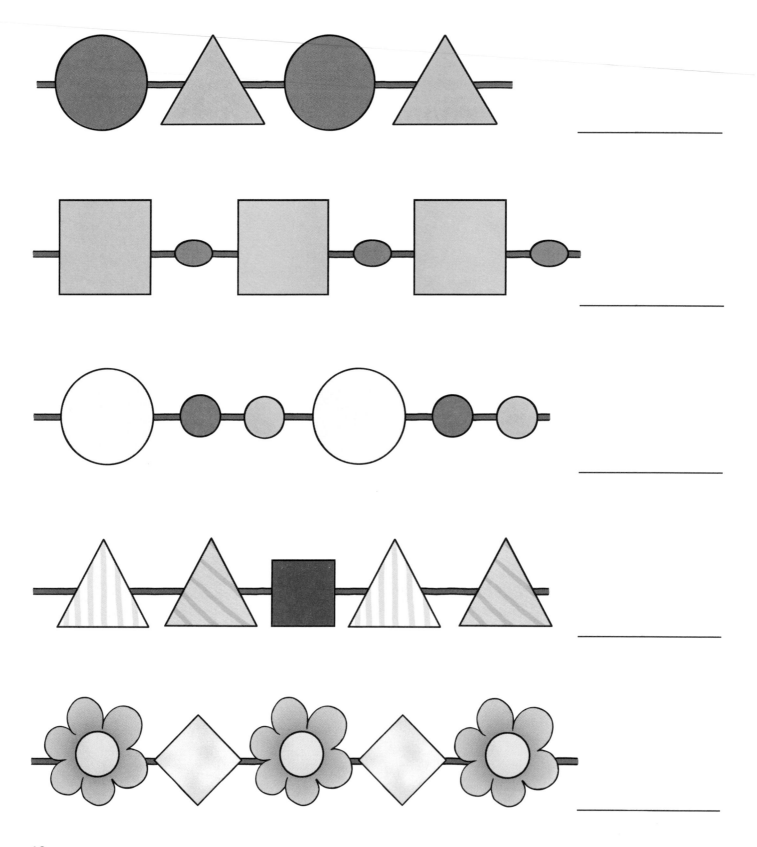

Identify and complete a pattern   © School Zone Publishing Company

What's Missing?

Draw the missing shapes on each string.

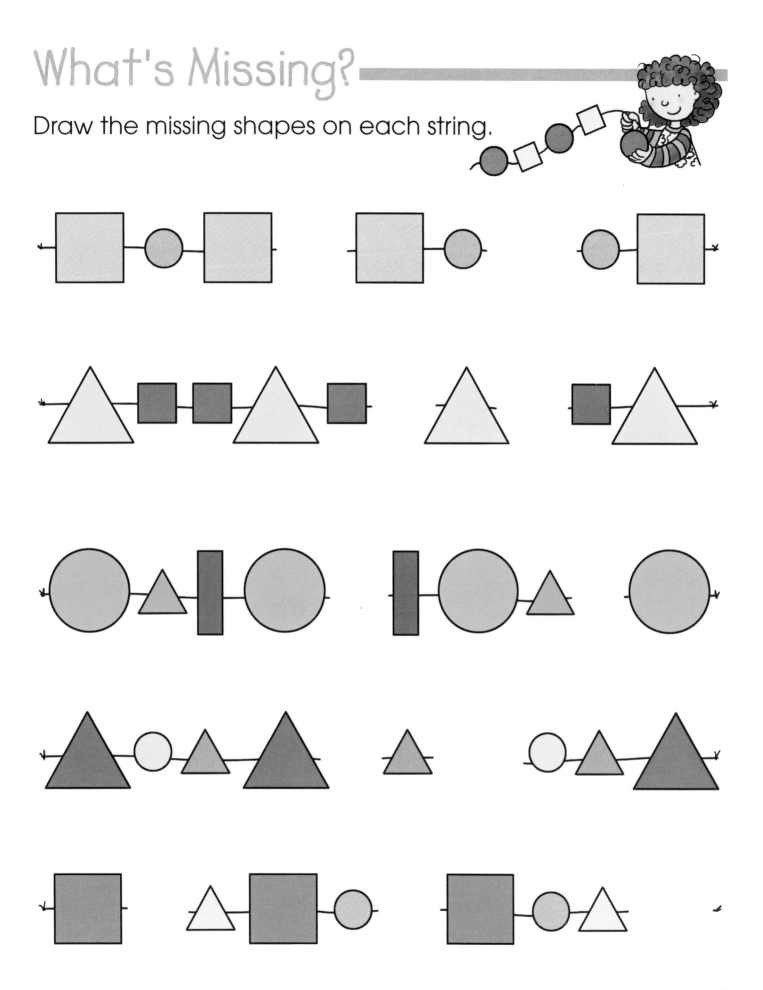

Two Parts

Each shape has two parts.
Some shapes have equal size parts.

equal parts   **parts are not equal size**

Circle the shapes that have equal size parts.

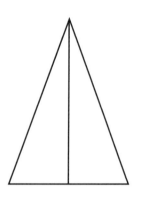 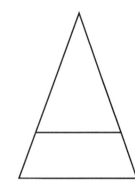 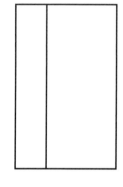 

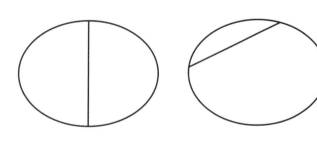 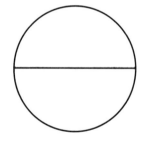 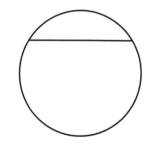

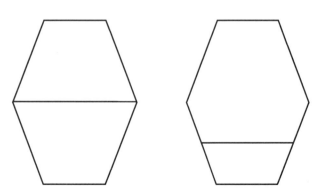 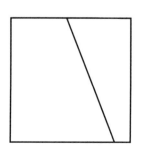 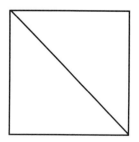

Shapes with equal and unequal parts

One-Half

Each of these shapes has two equal parts.
Each part is $\frac{1}{2}$ of the whole.

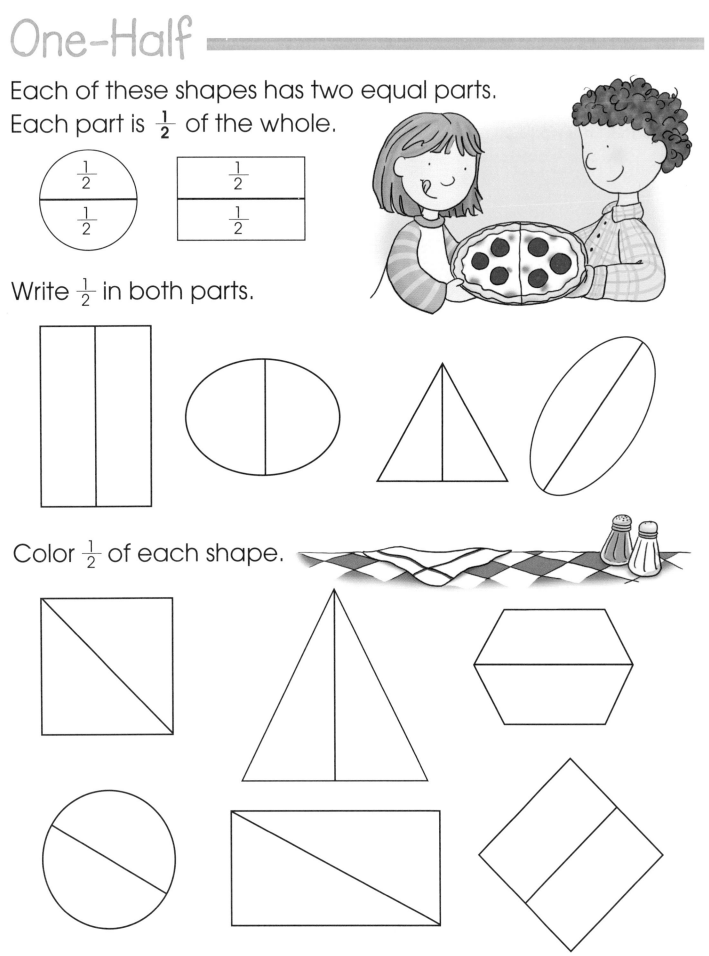

Write $\frac{1}{2}$ in both parts.

Color $\frac{1}{2}$ of each shape.

Fractions; concept of *one-half*   43

Tell Time

A clock has two hands.
The **little** hand points to the **hours**.
The **big** hand points to the **minutes**.

Write the **time** below each clock.

3:00

Same Time

Draw lines to connect the clocks that tell the **same time**.

Show the Time

Look at the time below each clock.
Draw a little hand on the clock to match.

2:00

4:00

9:00

11:00

Find the Time

How many clocks say **4:00**? _____

How many clocks say **9:00**? _____

Identify and count clocks   47

The Penny

front   back

A **penny** is **one cent**.

1 penny = **1¢**

How many cents are there?
Write each amount on the line.

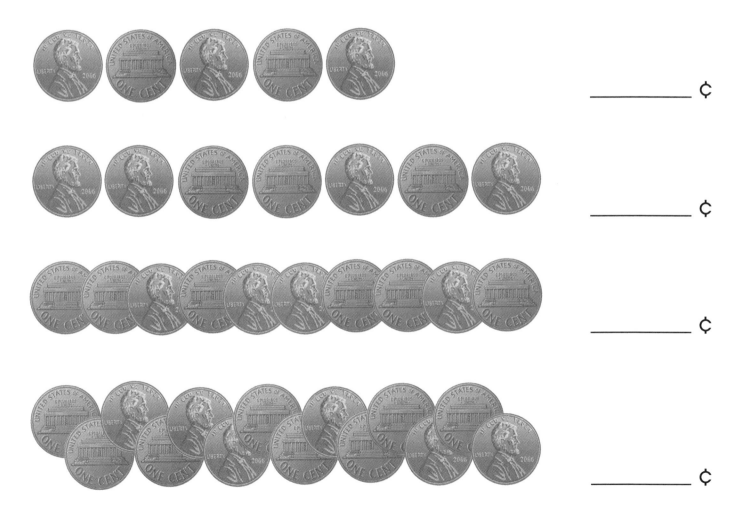

_____ ¢

_____ ¢

_____ ¢

_____ ¢

Count Money

Count the money in each purse.
Write the amount for each set.
Circle the amount that is **greater**.

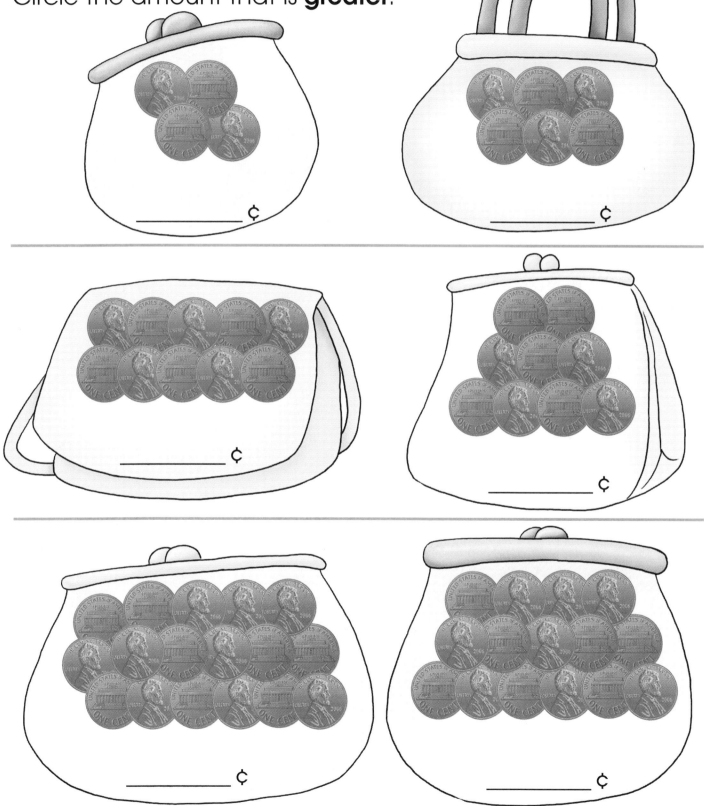

_____ ¢

_____ ¢

_____ ¢

_____ ¢

_____ ¢

_____ ¢

The Nickel

front   back

A **nickel** is **five cents**.

1 nickel = **5¢**

How many cents are there?
Write each amount on the line.

_____ ¢

_____ ¢

_____ ¢

Count Money

Count the money in each purse.
Write the amount for each set.
Circle the amount that is **greater**.

_____ ¢

_____ ¢

_____ ¢

_____ ¢

_____ ¢

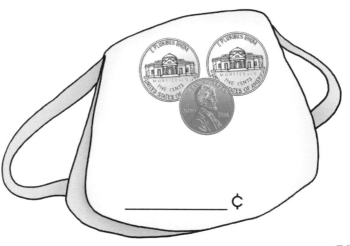

_____ ¢

Count money—pennies and nickels; compare amounts

The Dime

front   back

A **dime** is **ten cents**.

1 dime = **10¢**

BEE'S BEST HONEY   10¢

How many cents are there?
Write each amount on the line.

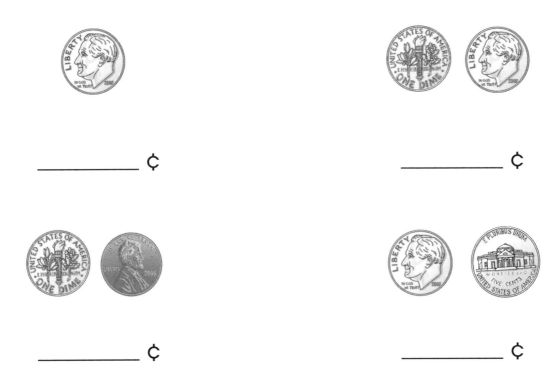

_____ ¢   _____ ¢

_____ ¢   _____ ¢

Count Money

Count the money.
Write the amount on the line.

_____ ¢

_____ ¢

_____ ¢

_____ ¢

_____ ¢

_____ ¢

Count money—pennies, nickels, and dimes

How Much Money?

Count the money.
Write the amount on the line.

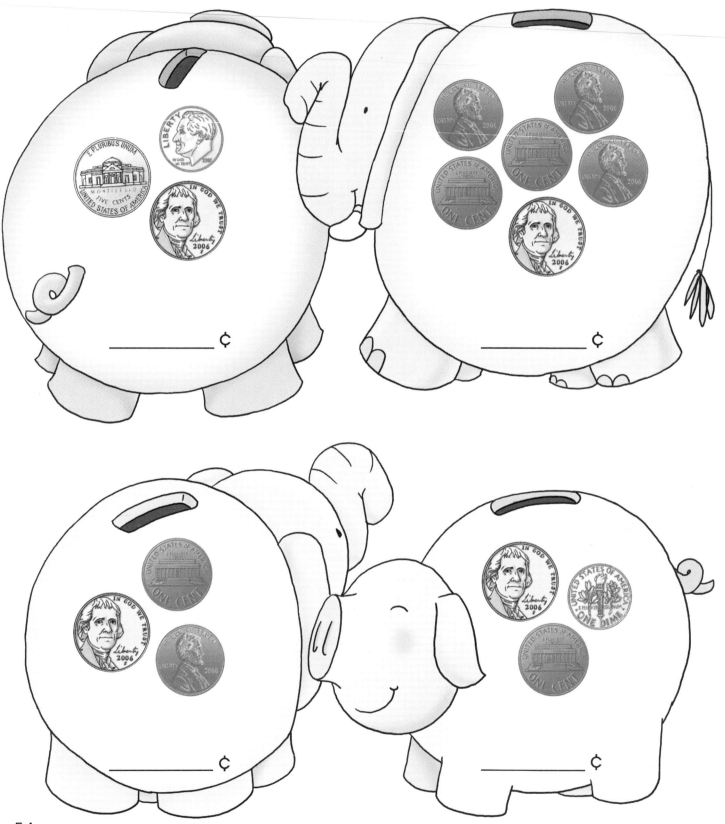

_____ ¢

_____ ¢

_____ ¢

_____ ¢

Count money-pennies, nickels, and dimes

How Much Does It Cost?

Count the money. Write each amount.
Draw a line from the amount to the toy you can buy.

_____ ¢

_____ ¢

_____ ¢

_____ ¢

What I Learned About Numbers

How many are there in each set?
Write the number in the box.

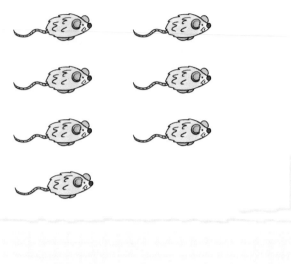

Write the missing numbers.

0 1 ___ ___ 4 ___

___ ___ 17 ___ 19 ___

Which number comes **before**?

_____ 14 15   _____ 6 7   _____ 1 2

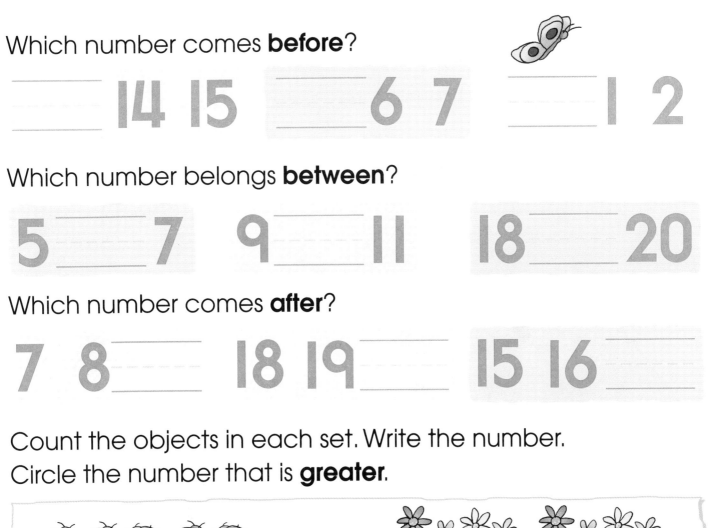

Which number belongs **between**?

5 _____ 7   9 _____ 11   18 _____ 20

Which number comes **after**?

7 8 _____   18 19 _____   15 16 _____

Count the objects in each set. Write the number.
Circle the number that is **greater**.

_____   _____

Circle the number that is **greater**.

7 5   16 19   17 15

Circle the number that is **less**.

20 12   17 13   9 0

Review numbers 0–20

What I Learned About...

Match the shape to the picture.

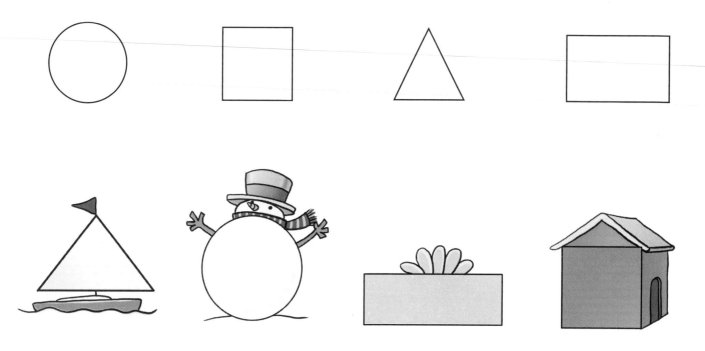

What comes next?

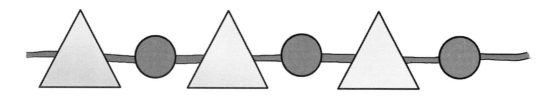

_____

Circle the shapes that have equal size parts.
Write $\frac{1}{2}$ on each part of those shapes.

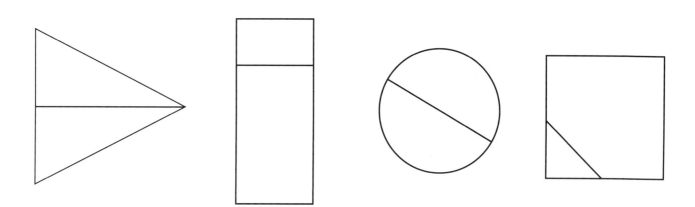

Shapes, Time, and Money

Write the **time** on the line.

Draw the little hand.

_____

_____

4:00

How many cents are there?
Write the amount on the line.

_____ ¢

_____ ¢

Answer Key

Page 1

0
1
2
3
4
5

Page 2

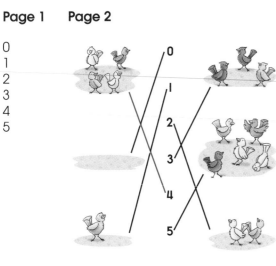

0
1
2
3
4
5

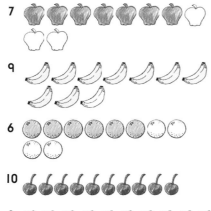

Page 3

3   1
5   0
2   4

Page 4

6
7
8
9
10

Page 5

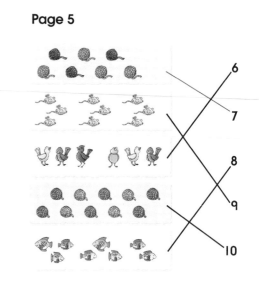

6
7
8
9
10

Page 6

5   7
6   9
10 8

Page 7

7

9

6

10

8

Page 8

Page 9

Count	Color	Write
		7
		3
		9
		5
		8
		6

Page 10

0 1 2 **3** 4 5 **6**
0 1 **2** 3 **4 5** 6
3 4 **5** 6 7 8 **9**
4 **5 6** 7 8 9 **10**
4 5 6 **7 8 9** 10

Page 11

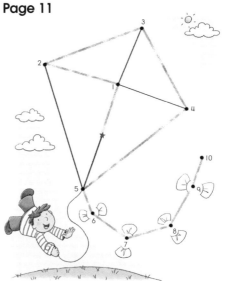

Page 12

3
9
8
8

60   Answer key

Page 13

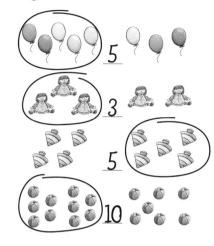

5

3

5

10

Page 14

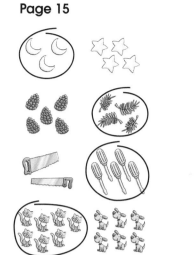

Page 15

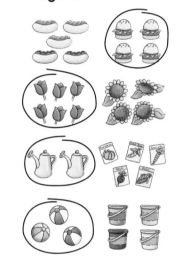

Page 16

2   3
5
8
7

Page 17

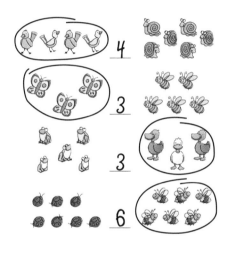

4

3

3

6

Page 18

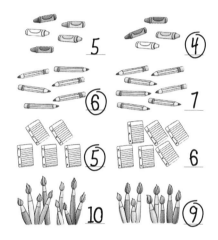

5   ④

⑥   1

⑤   6

10   ⑨

Page 19

Page 20

11
12
13
14
15

Page 21

12   15
14   13

Page 22

16
17
18
19
20

Page 23

17   19
20   18

Page 24

Page 25

Count	Color	Write
		16
		18
		10
		15
		17

Page 26

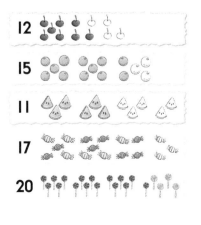

12

15

11

17

20

Page 27

3   11
5   8
2   15

Page 28

8   13
10   12
9   16

Page 29

15   5
19   10
12   8

Page 30

5 **6 7** 8 **9** 10
6 **7** 8 **9 10** 11
10 **11 12** 13 **14** 15
13 **14 15** 16 **17** 18
15 16 17 **18** 19 **20**

Page 31

Page 32

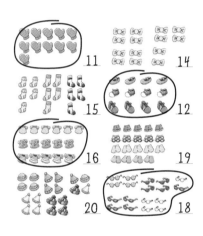

Page 33

13 XXXXXXXXXXX XXX

15 XXXXXXXXX XXXX

12 XXXXXXXXXX XX

17 XXXXXXXXXX XXXXXXX

7 XXXXXXX

9 XXXXXXXXX

10 XXXXXXXXXX

19 XXXXXXXXXX XXXXXXXX

Page 34

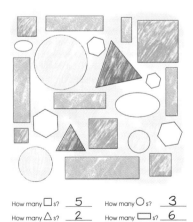

Page 35

9 XXXXXXXXX

7 XXXXXXX

6 XXXXXX

17 XXXXXXXXXX XXXXXXX

13 XXXXXXXXXX XXX

19 XXXXXXXXXX XXXXXXXXX

15 XXXXXXXXXX XXXXX

14 XXXXXXXXXX XXXX

Page 36

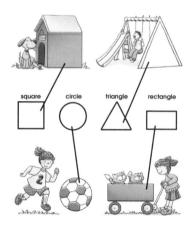

square   circle   triangle   rectangle

Page 37

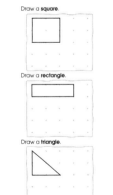

How many ☐ s? _5_   How many ◯ s? _3_
How many △ s? _2_   How many ▭ s? _6_

Page 38

Answers can vary

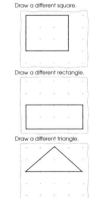

Draw a **square**.
Draw a different square.
Draw a **rectangle**.
Draw a different rectangle.
Draw a **triangle**.
Draw a different triangle.

Page 39

Write **c** on each ◯. How many ◯ s? _8_
Write **t** on each △. How many △ s? _7_
Write **s** on each ☐. How many ☐ s? _4_

Page 40

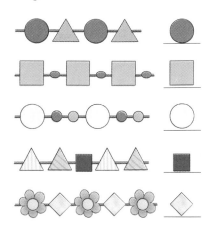

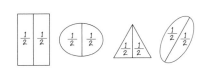

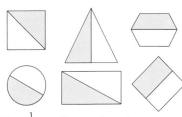

Page 41

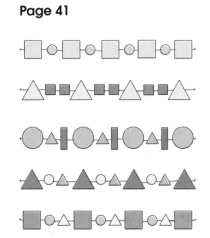

Page 42

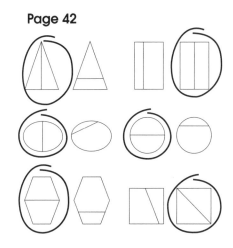

Page 43

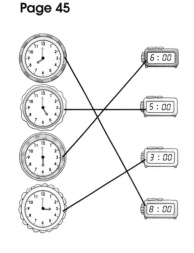

The $\frac{1}{2}$ section colored can vary.

Page 44

7:00   12:00
1:00   10:00

Page 45

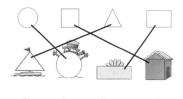

Page 46

2:00   4:00

9:00   11:00

Page 47

How many clocks say **4:00**? __8__
How many clocks say **9:00**? __7__

Page 48

5¢
7¢
10¢
14¢

Page 50

10¢
15¢
20¢

Page 52

10¢   20¢
11¢   15¢

Page 54

20¢   10¢
7¢   16¢

Page 49

4¢   6¢
(circle 6¢)
10¢   9¢
(circle 10¢)
17¢   15¢
(circle 17¢)

Page 51

8¢   6¢
(circle 8¢)
7¢   10¢
(circle 10¢)
15¢   11¢
(circle 15¢)

Page 53

13¢
17¢
20¢
15¢
17¢
20¢

Page 55

20¢ Duck

11¢ Gum

15¢ Ball

12¢
Spinner Top

Page 56

7   13
0   20

0 1 **2 3** 4 **5 6**
15 16 17 **18** 19 **20**

Page 57

13 5   0
6   10 19
9   20 17
13 16 (Circle 16)
7   19 17
12 13 0

Page 58

Page 59

8:00

18¢   17¢

Award

Great Job!

_____
Name

finished Transition Math

from

School Zone Publishing.

   02207 Transition Math K–1